MW01435809

Welcome back to ST. THOMAS

ALEX WILSON
ILLUSTRATED BY MATTHEW DUNHAM

Welcome Back to St. Thomas
Copyright © 2024 by Alex Wilson

All rights reserved. No part of this publication may be reproduced, distributed, or transmitted in any form or by any means, including photocopying, recording, or other electronic or mechanical methods, without the prior written permission of the author, except in the case of brief quotations embodied in critical reviews and certain other non-commercial uses permitted by copyright law.

tellwell
Tellwell Talent
www.tellwell.ca

ISBN
978-0-2288-9403-2 (Hardcover)
978-0-2288-9402-5 (Paperback)

To my son Wilsey, and my hometown St. Thomas.

Tomorrow we'll visit some family we haven't seen in a while. Can I tell you some things about the city that will make you smile?

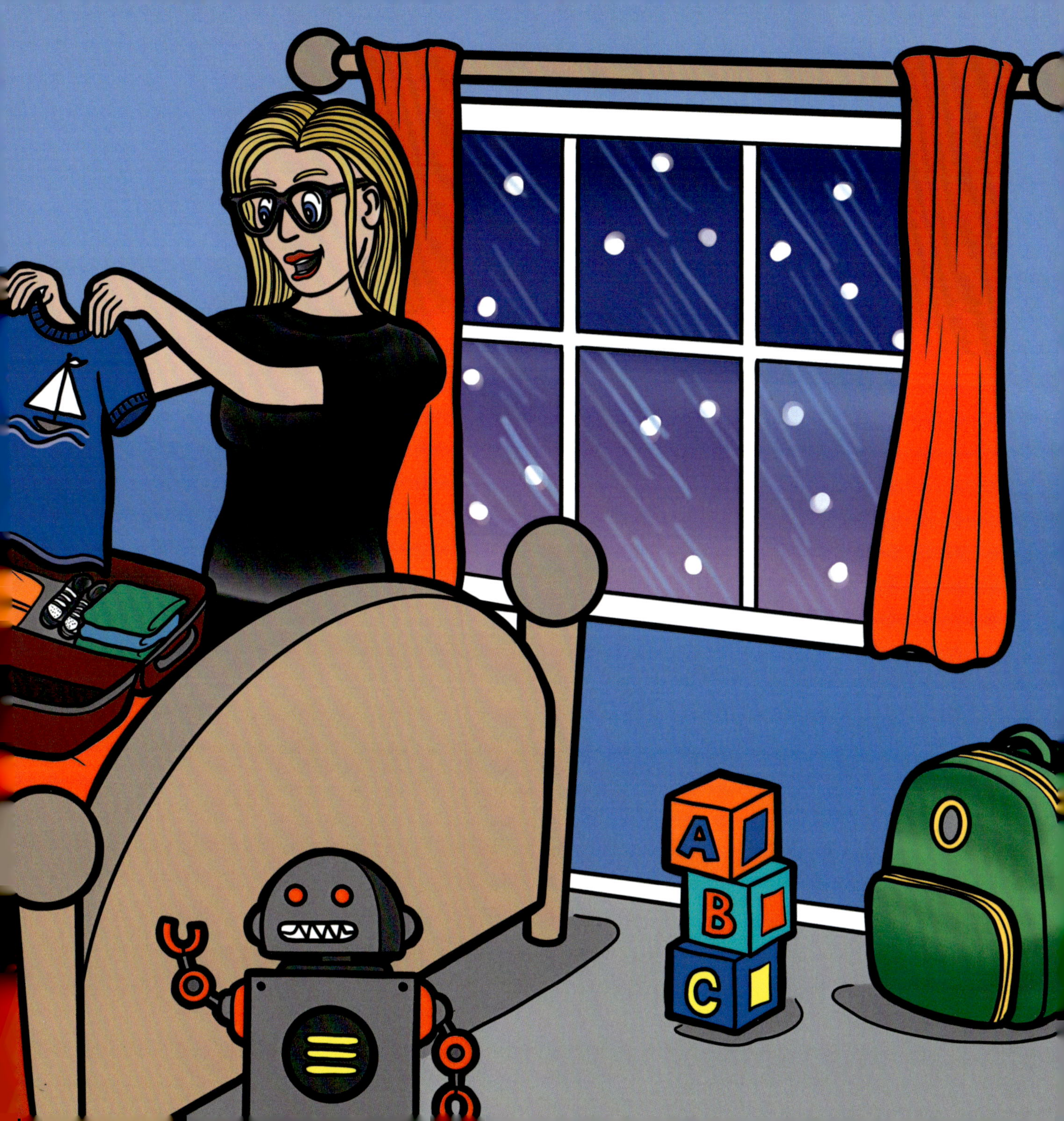
A
B
C

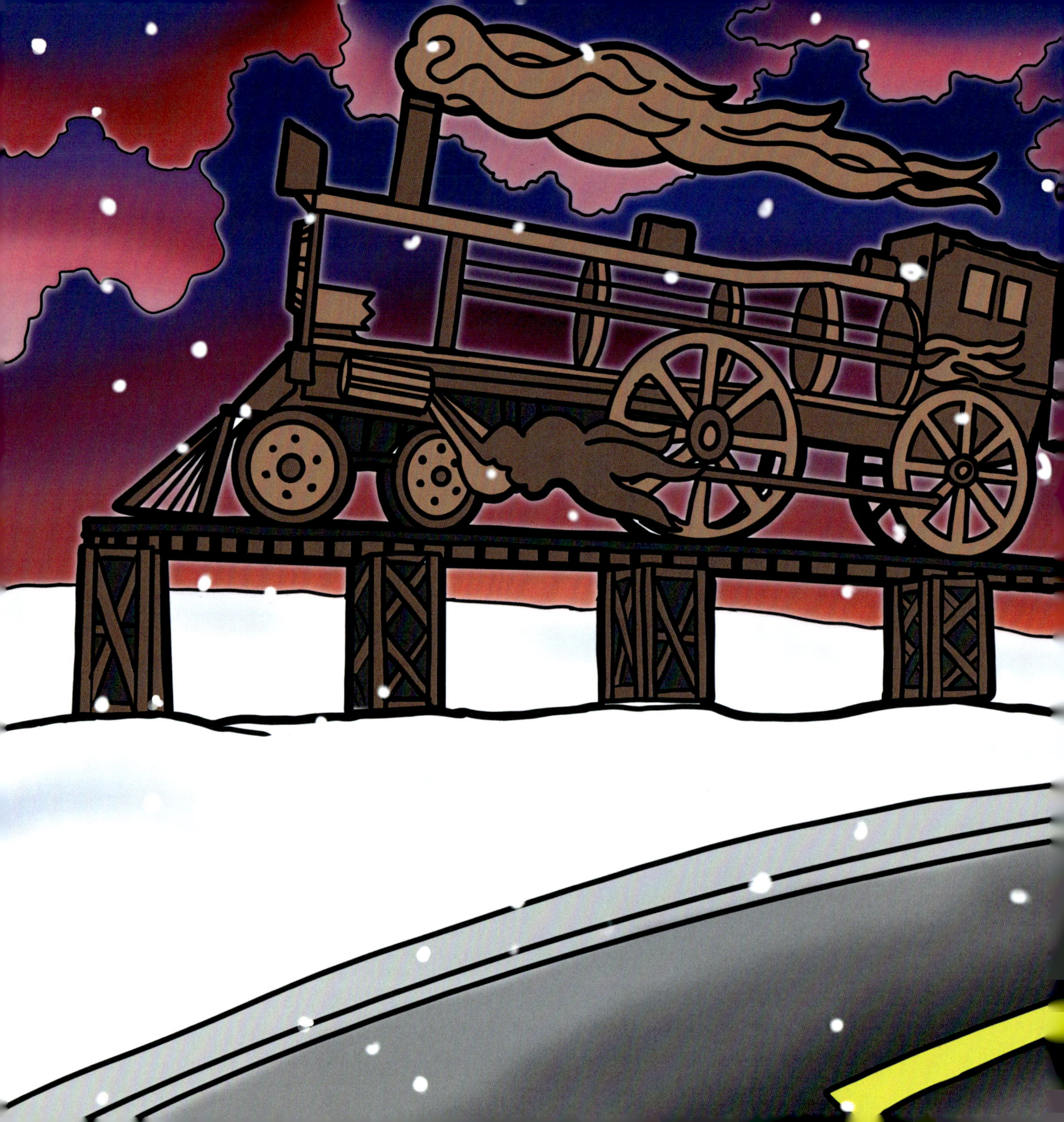

Surrounded by farmers' fields is a place we know as St.T. It's where I was born, where I was raised, and where I became me.

ST. THOMAS

ST.THOMAS

THE RAILWAY CI

KING BURGER
24hr DRIVE THRU
RED & WHITE PIZZA
PLAYPLA
Mc WILSEYS
DRIVE THRU

Let's drive down the main drag also known as Talbot Street. It's a great road for cruising and getting something quick to eat.

TACO LAND

W-DINER RESTAURANT

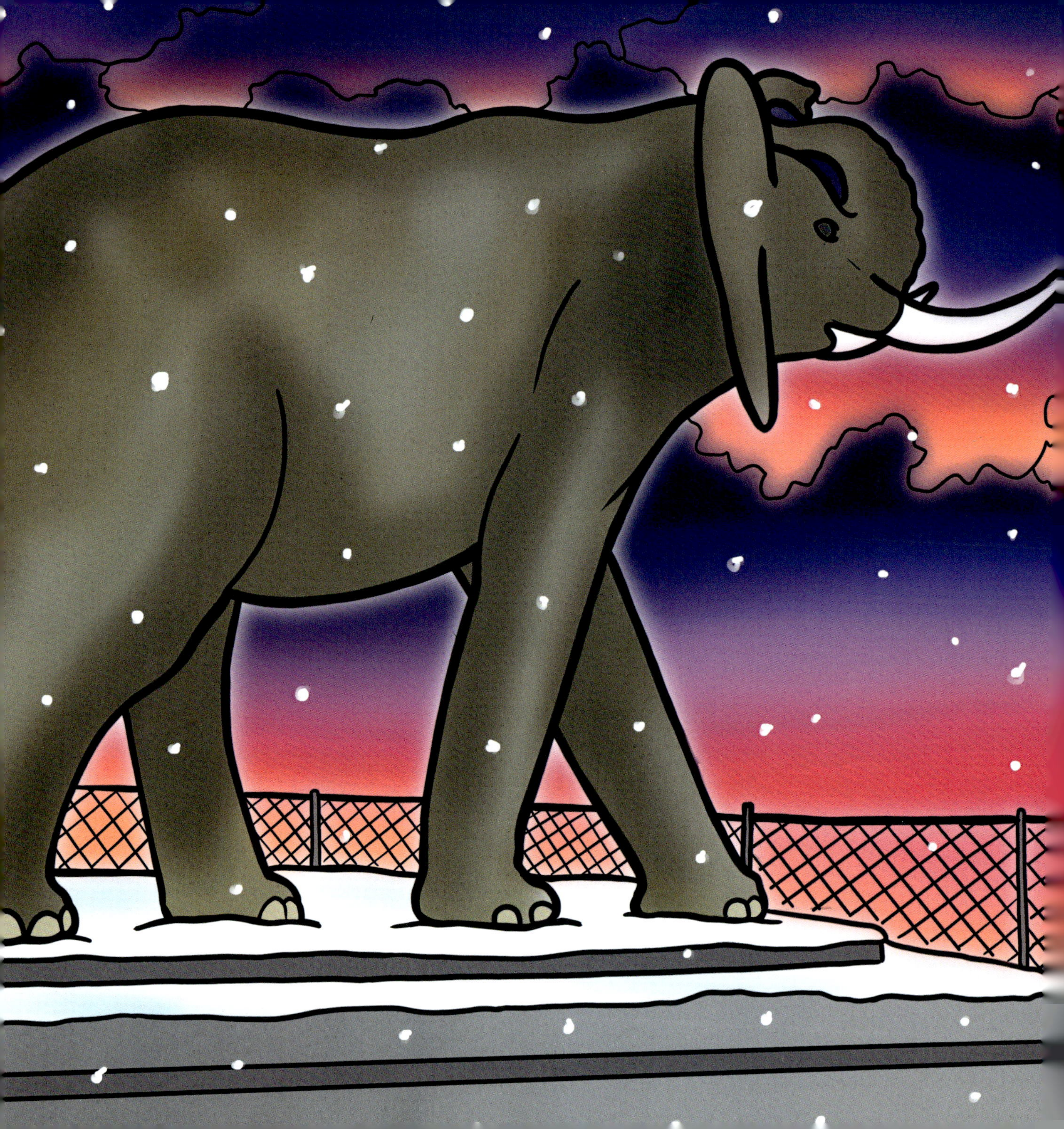

One of my first memories was seeing Jumbo the Elephant at his impressive height. Always standing proudly and watching over the community at night.

Just down the road they built the Elevated Park where we liked to explore. Do you remember? You've been many times before.

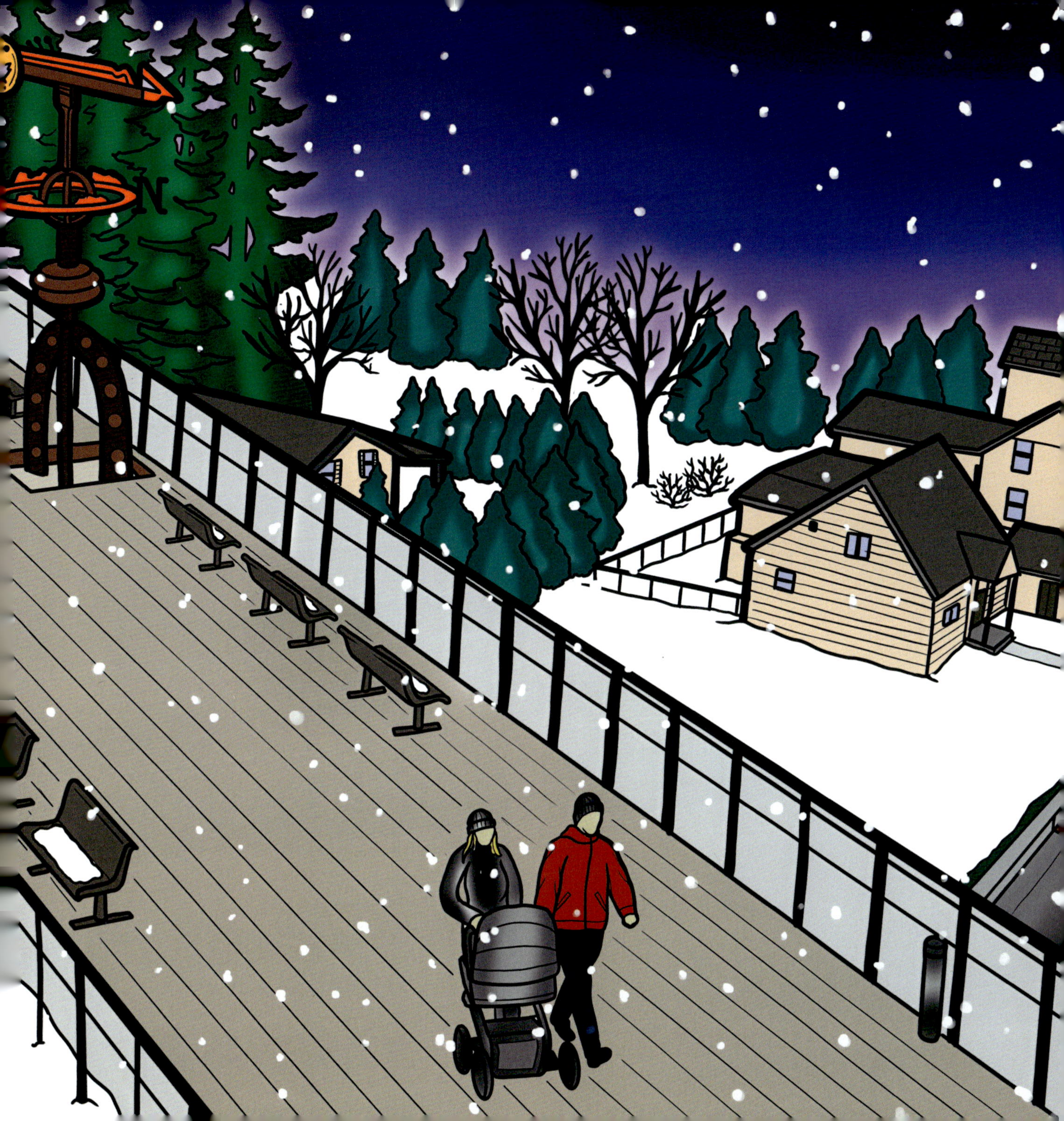
N

Listen closely to the bell at City Hall saying, "I'm still awake!" It chimes every hour and believe me kid, it's never had a break.

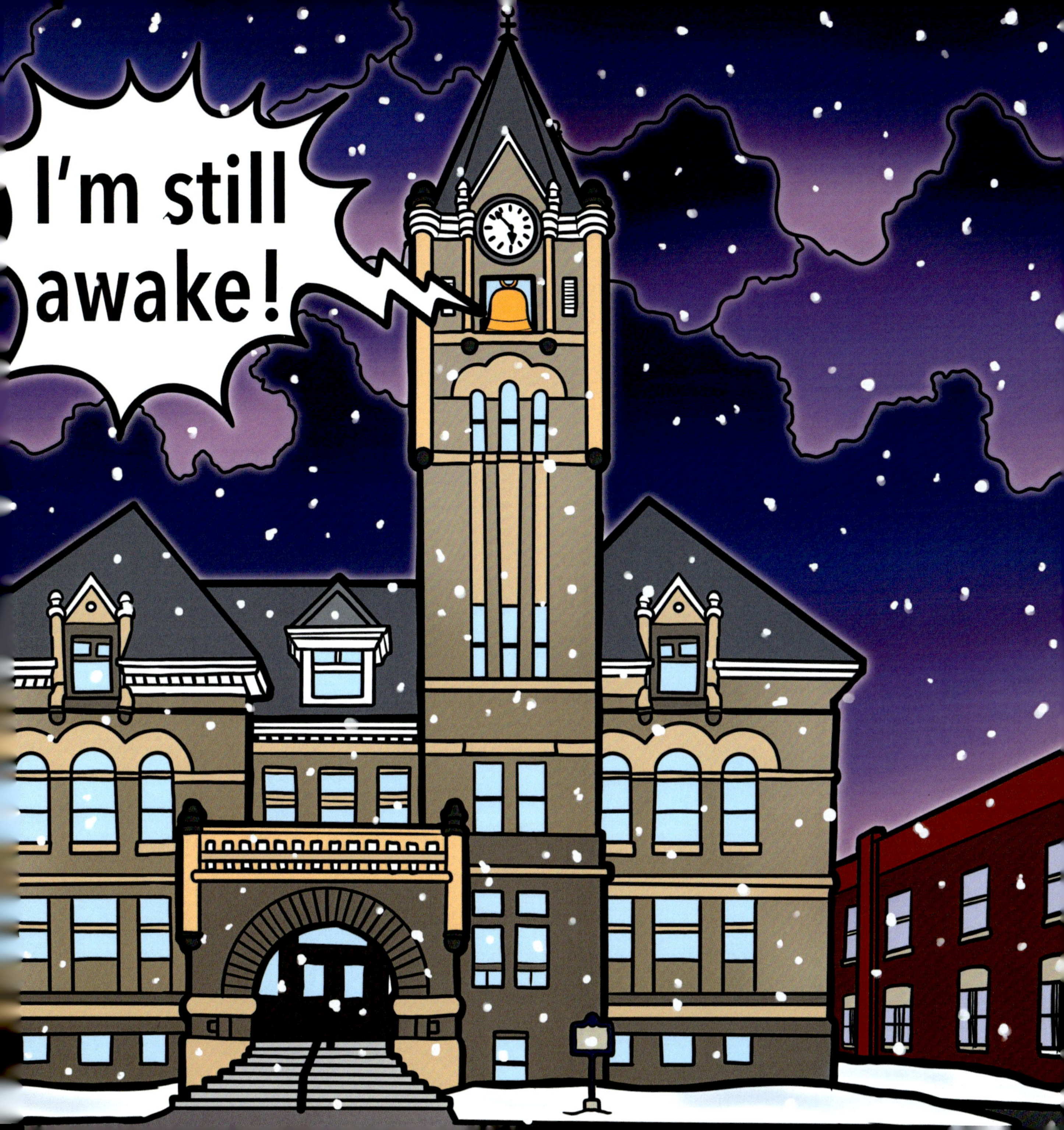
I'm still awake!

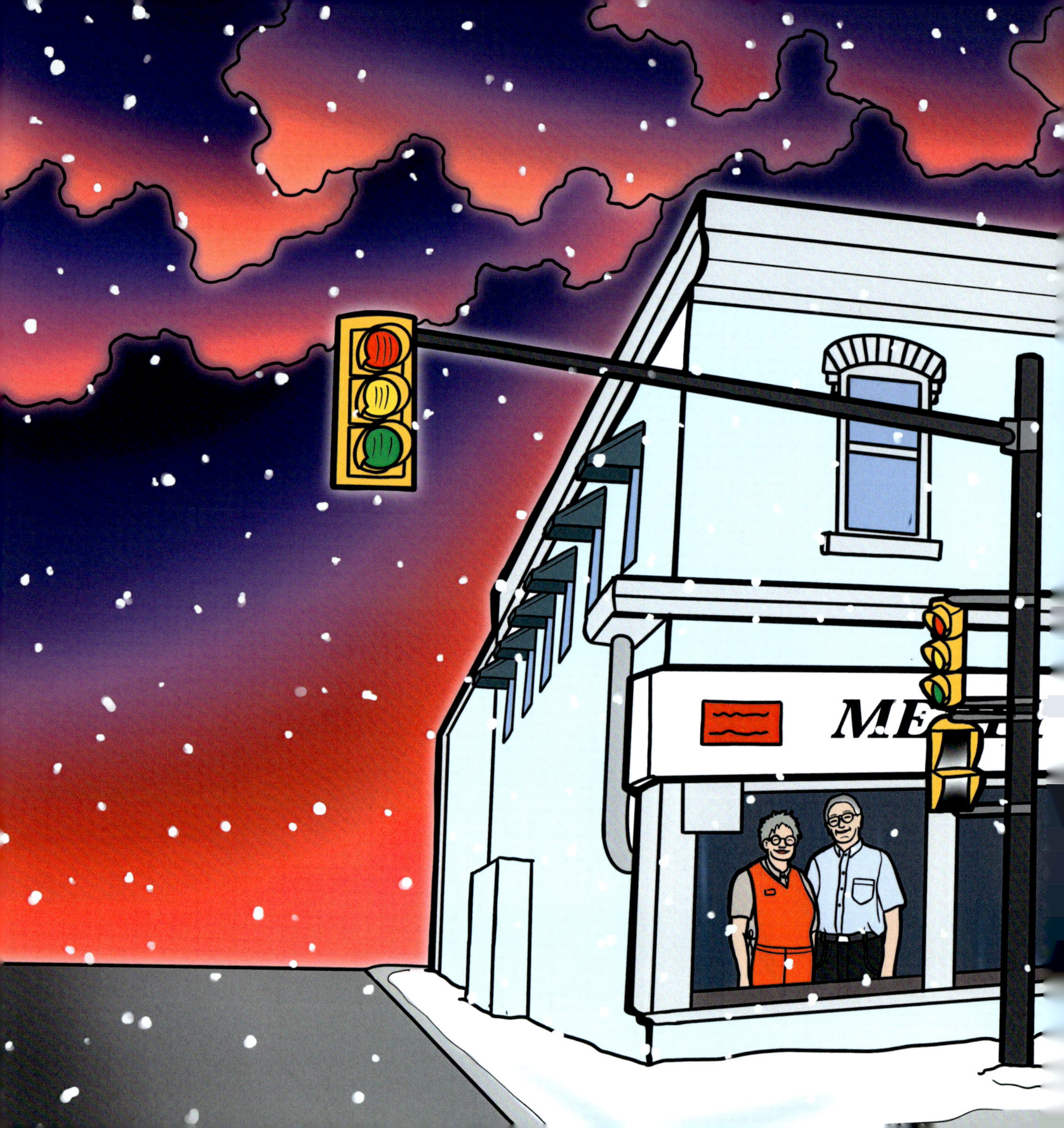

Years ago, your great-grandparents owned a local hardware store. Now that I'm older, I miss everything about it so much more.

RO HARDWARE

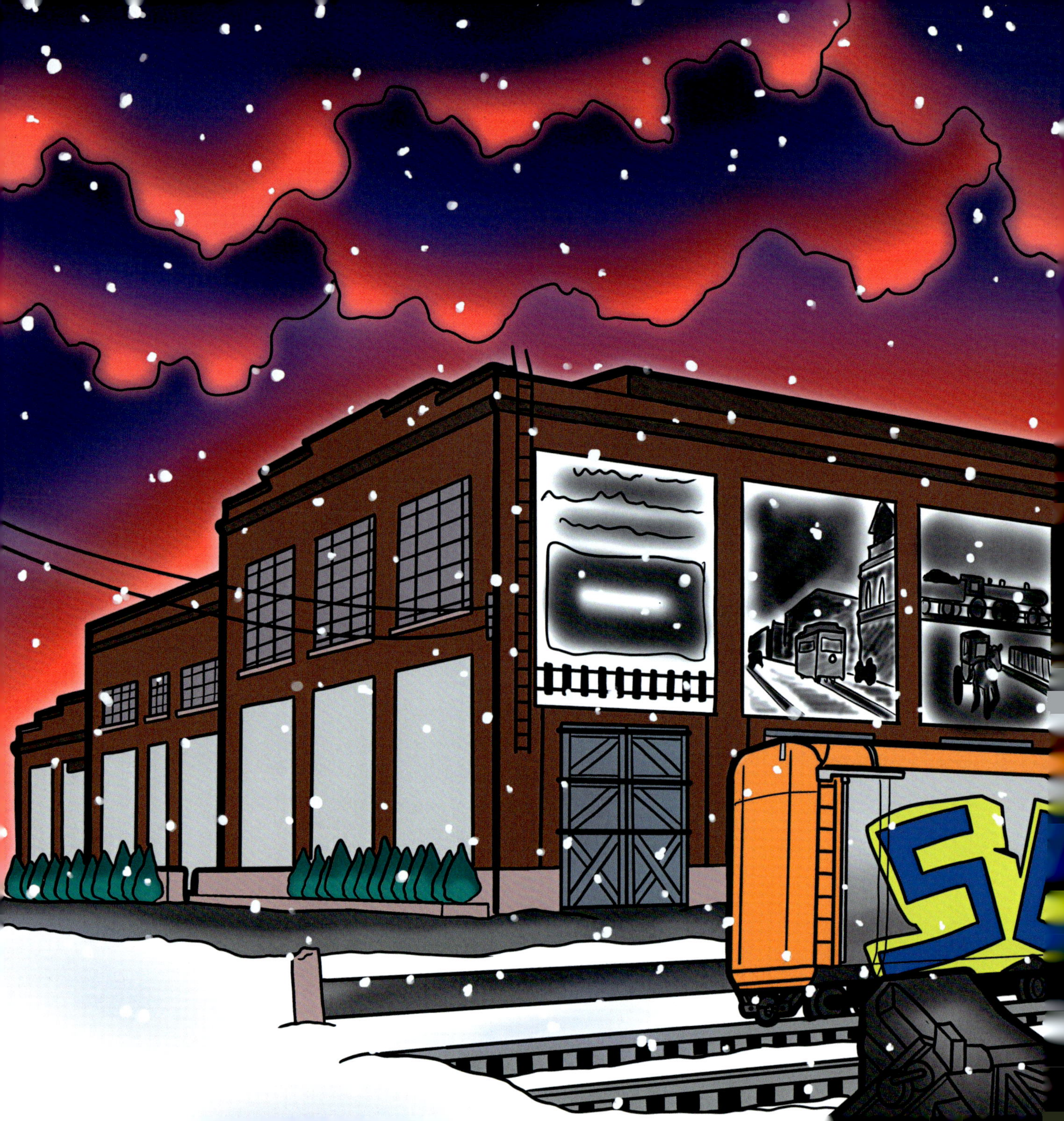

Did you know this town is known for the railways and beautiful art? There are always trains resting on the tracks before their time to depart.

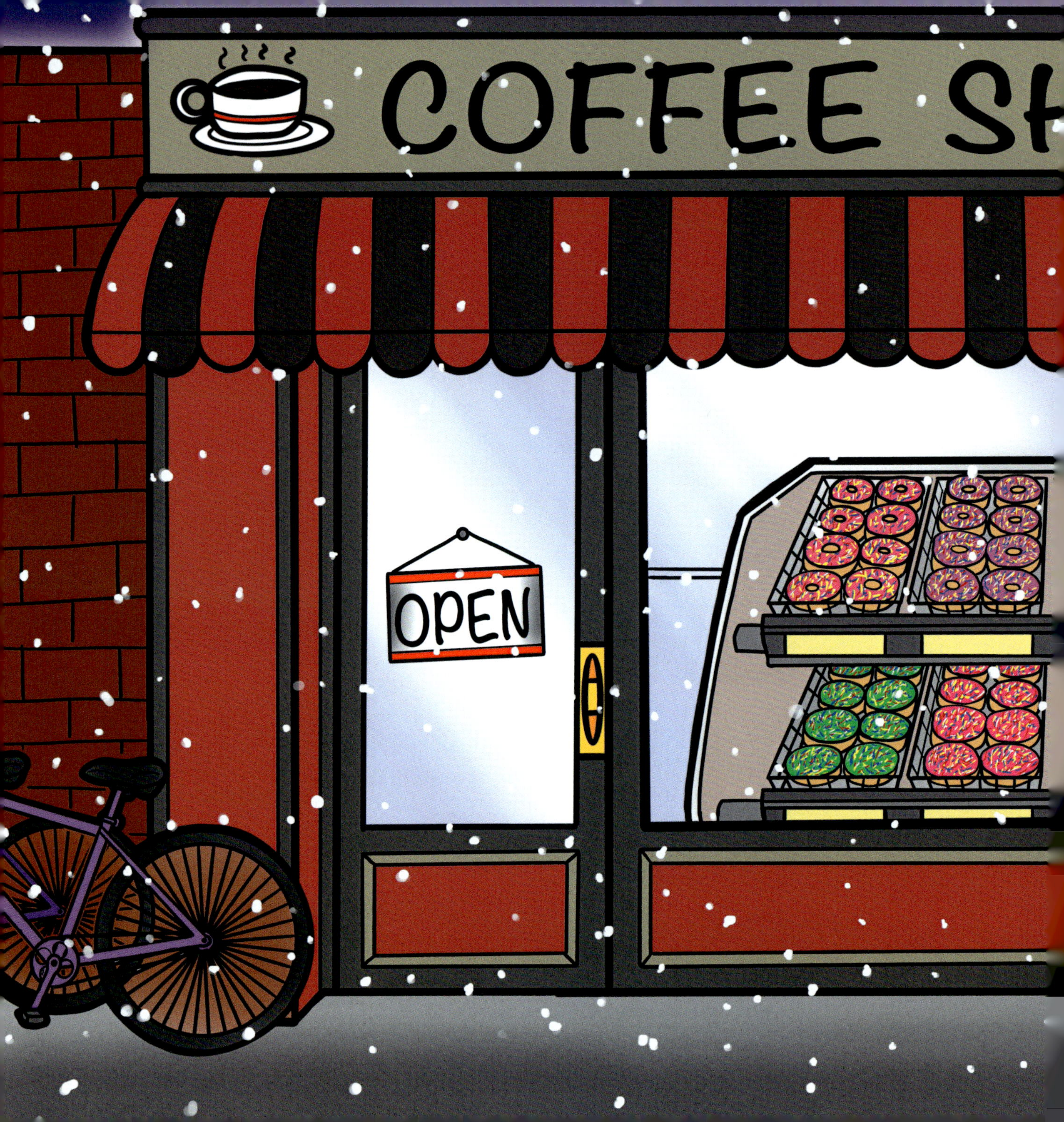
COFFEE SH
OPEN

When we got our fun money and were craving donuts and refreshing pops, We'd race our bikes down to one of the many twenty-four-hour coffee shops.

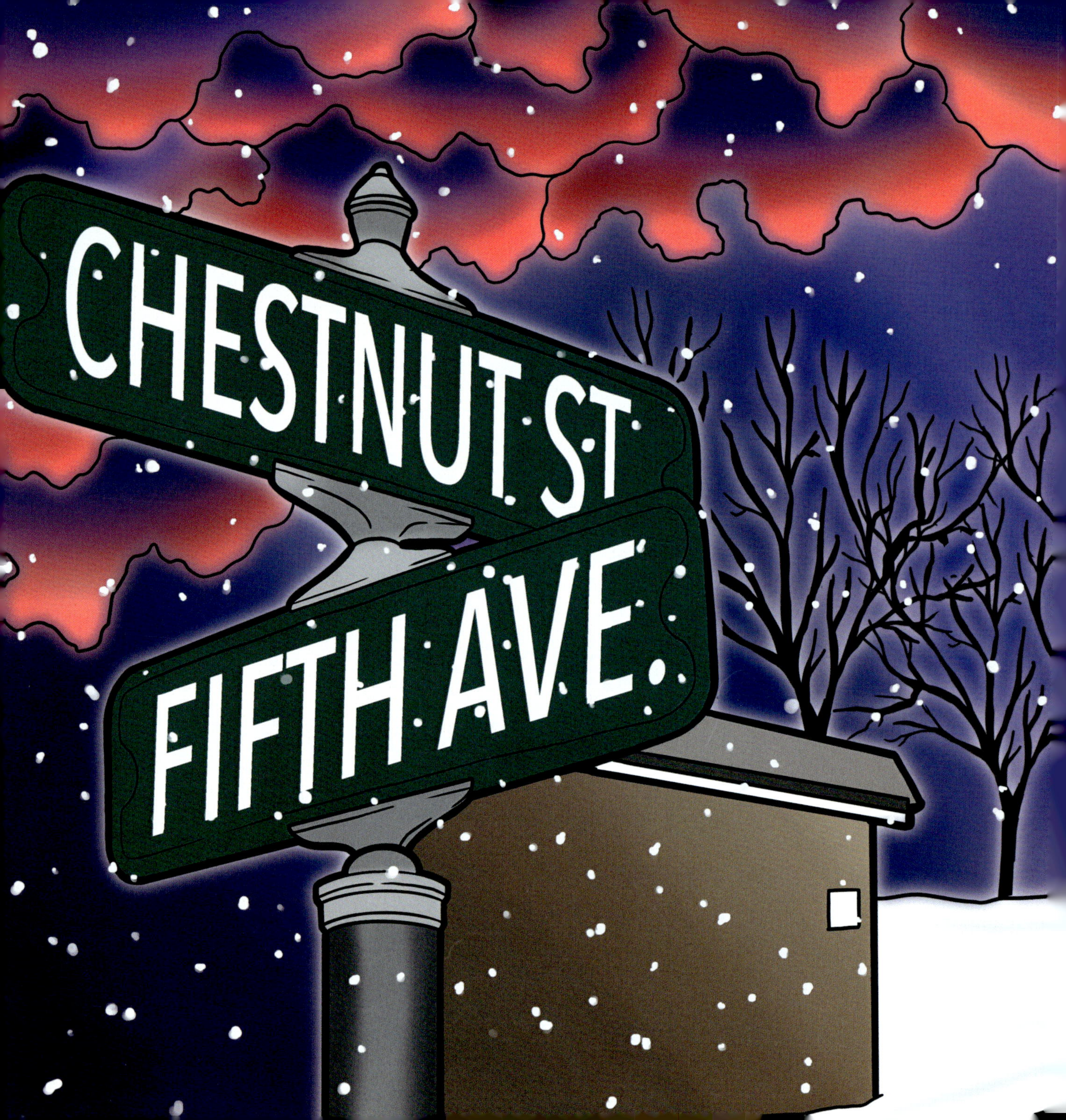
CHESTNUT ST
FIFTH AVE.

Classic Chestnut Street Hill was a good spot to bring the sleds. Always being careful we wore helmets and didn't bump our heads.

Do you remember our family reunion down at Pinafore Park? In the winter there are Christmas lights so families can explore after dark.

tasy of Lights

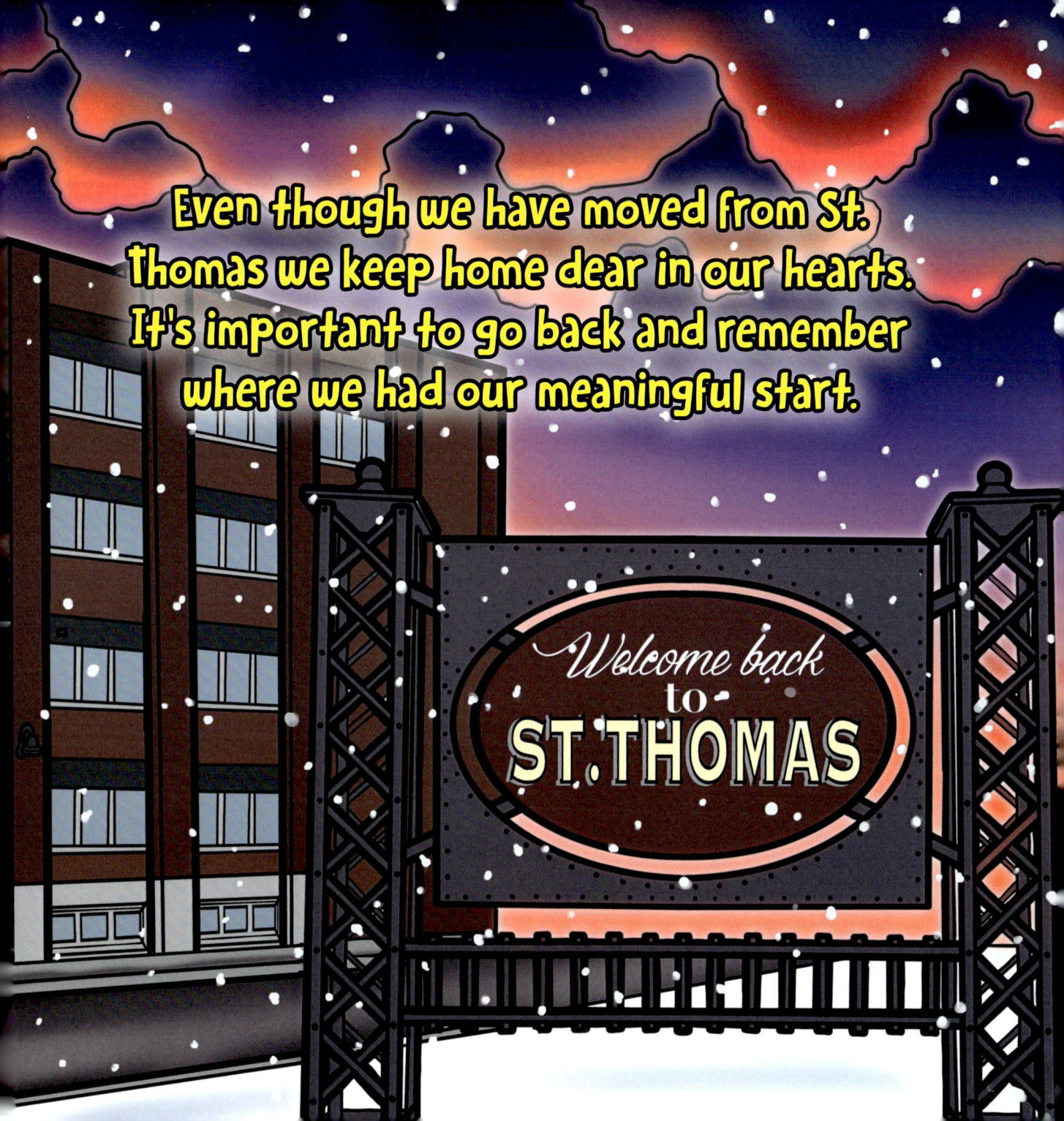

Even though we have moved from St. Thomas we keep home dear in our hearts. It's important to go back and remember where we had our meaningful start.

About the Author

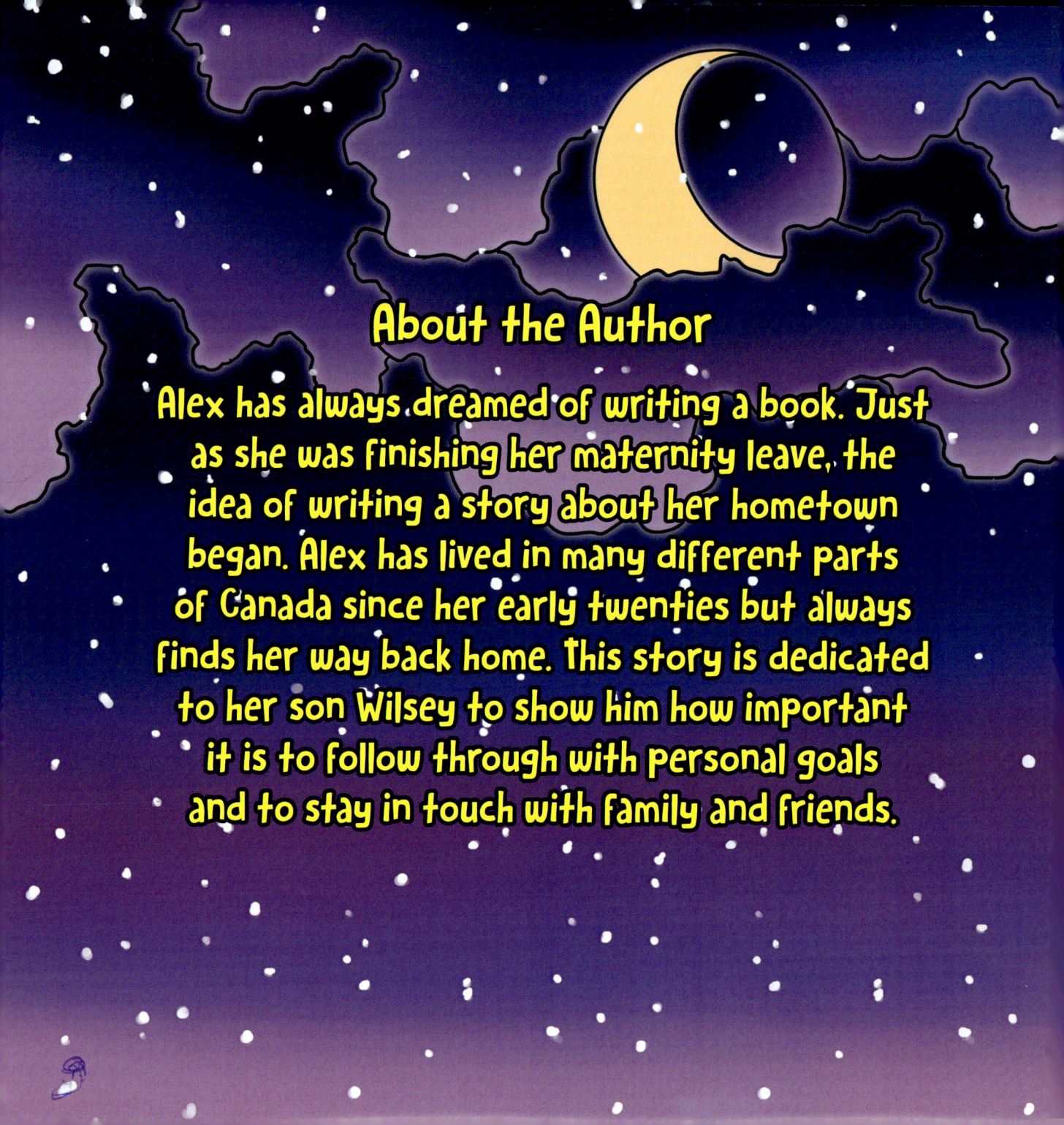

Alex has always dreamed of writing a book. Just as she was finishing her maternity leave, the idea of writing a story about her hometown began. Alex has lived in many different parts of Canada since her early twenties but always finds her way back home. This story is dedicated to her son Wilsey to show him how important it is to follow through with personal goals and to stay in touch with family and friends.